"Sunny Kaila's journey took him from a farming village in India to building hugely successful technology businesses in America, and his story is one of the clearest examples of 10x thinking I've ever seen. In Borderless Life, Sunny doesn't just reflect on where he's been; he also provides a blueprint for where you can go, too. He teaches you how to recognize the borders you've accepted in your business, relationships, health, and mindset, and how to break through them with intention, capability, and purpose. The entrepreneurs of the future will be borderless—like Sunny. Will you join him?"

—Dan Sullivan
Co-Founder of Strategic Coach® Inc.
Co-Author of *Who Not How, The Gap and The Gain,*
and *10x is Easier than 2x*

"Sunny embodies Borderless Life. His value creation is not limited by geography, language, or culture. His proven process is evidenced by his tangible international impact. Read this book and you'll learn how to play a bigger game."

—Dr. Kary Oberbrunner
Wall Street Journal and *USA Today* Bestselling Author

BORDERLESS LIFE

HOW TO BUILD YOUR EVER-EXPANDING FUTURE

BORDERLESS LIFE

HOW TO BUILD YOUR EVER-EXPANDING FUTURE

SUNNY KAILA

ethos
collective

Printed in the United States of America

Published by Igniting Souls
PO Box 43, Powell, OH 43065
IgnitingSouls.com

LCCN: 2025911719
Paperback ISBN: 978-1-63680-526-9
Hardback ISBN: 978-1-63680-527-6
eBook ISBN: 978-1-63680-528-3

Available in paperback, hardcover, e-book, and audiobook.

Table of Contents

Part 1: My Borderless Life

Part 2: Breaking Borders

Part 3: Your Borderless Life

PART 1

My Borderless Life

1

Taxi to Tech

Vision for a Borderless Future

Everyone has borders.

They manifest shortly after birth in the form of perceived limitations to what each person can achieve in life based on their family, country, mental and physical capabilities, financial status, and more. As a child grows, these imposed borders only become stronger as societal influences dictate what each person can or cannot do.

My life began the same way. I was born in a farming village in India, and my borders arrived soon after. Farmers in India, especially in remote villages, cannot make enough money to live a comfortable life, and my circumstances were already shepherding me toward that fate. Long before I could understand what was going on, a financial border had limited my life potential.

Similarly, I faced an educational border simply because I had limited access to quality education. For most of my childhood, I remained within these borders, knowing they weren't right but accepting their reality. When I turned seventeen, I wanted to attend medical school, but there were no medical colleges in my area, and I felt that my ignorance of the English language and lack of quality education would hold me back.

Does this sound familiar? Has your life been defined by limits you never created and circumstances you can't control? The good news is that freedom from these borders is possible. My life has proven it over and over.

The first border I consciously and intentionally broke was geographical. I decided to explore opportunities beyond my village borders. As I saw it, I had three options: I could move to Russia and study at a medical college, travel to the U.S. and seek a blue-collar career, or remain in India.

In a step of courage and faith, I wrote each country's name on a slip of paper—United States, India, and Russia—folded them, and placed them in front of me as I prayed at my local Gurudwara (Sikh temple). I decided I would choose one of the slips of paper at random, guided only by my Ardas (prayers). Whichever I picked would determine my destination and the course of my life.

I happened to select America.

From Farm Land to Foreign Land

At eighteen years old, I had just arrived in New York City. I stood on the New Jersey side, looking at Lady Liberty. I didn't know any English, and I didn't even have enough money for the ferry ticket to go to Liberty Island. Despite the sadness and uncertainty, my future was wide open, and I embraced the freedom before me with excitement.

I started out pumping gas for a year before it was time to expand my capabilities. I got my taxi license and became a cab driver in New York City. My income doubled, and so did my English, thanks to hundreds of conversations with passengers, even those who didn't want to talk to me.

It would have been easy to remain a taxi driver. I was making a solid $4,000 per month, and in time, I could have bought a gas station or another retail business. That was the typical route for immigrants from India, and I had friends who were following that exact route, saving up for a gas station, motel, or a Dunkin' Donuts.

But I didn't. Although it was a viable option for several of my friends, that route was a border for me, attempting to force me into one way of thinking. Instead, I chose to Think Borderless. I pursued further education instead.

I felt all the pressure of doubt. Would I be able to go to college? Even if I were accepted, it would cost me dearly. What if I couldn't acquire any financial aid or student loans? What's more, would I even be able to get a better job with the education I received? I had no guarantees, but I wouldn't let it hold me back.

I stopped by a community college to talk to an advisor there. That conversation gave me the edge I needed. It was 1995, and the internet was the newest phenomenon occupying everyone's minds. I realized if I was going to learn anything, it should be computers. My language barrier wouldn't be a liability—the native English speaker and I would be on level ground learning the new language of computers. I could negate the border.

I spent the next four years of my life breaking the taxi-driving border, studying for my computer engineering degree during the day and driving taxis from 5 p.m. to 5 a.m., seven days a week.

I had made it from taxi driver to tech professional after acquiring a job as a computer tech for a New York City advertising agency. I was making six figures, and I could have easily spent the rest of my life in that situation, but again, I was not yet borderless.

Although my life was comfortable, I had to pause and ask myself: "Is comfort really what I'm seeking? What do I want from life?" I realized that while pursuing a comfortable life was rational, it was a border, keeping me from more meaningful achievements.

I gathered my courage and took the next step. I launched my own IT company. As an entrepreneur, I woke up every morning unemployed, guided by no borders or limitations but my own ambition to grow my capabilities.

My company was an IT consulting service for small businesses in New York City. My income doubled again, but money was not the only important factor to consider. I started the business in 2003 when my wife and I had a newborn, but our second and third children soon joined us within six years. Working seven days a week was neither sustainable nor scalable. Time and space were my next borders.

So I brought my wife into the business. Now, I know what you're thinking. Why limit arguments to the home when you can have them at work as well, right? And yes, being business partners as well as life partners has strengthened our marriage to no end.

We hired four IT engineers to expand our business. Everything felt like a dream until I hit a new border: a relational one. All of a sudden, three of our four engineers left, taking fifty percent of our customers with them, nearly collapsing the business. I have long since learned that people don't leave bad companies; they leave bad relationships. I was a great engineer, but I struggled with relationships.

That's when a Punjabi proverb I learned from my father came back to me:

"Jindgi ch passae kamunae saukhe, changey bande kamuane aukhe." This translates to "It's easier to earn money in life than to earn good relationships."

I had two choices: allow this border to stop me and return to a full-time tech job, or stay, rebuild the business, and rethink my view of the importance of relationships.

We decided to fight for the business, but I knew we would have to reimagine everything from the ground up. The solution was simple but powerful. We doubled down on earning relationships and building collaborations until we began to thrive again. Changing my mindset so as not to diminish the importance of authentic relationships broke the border surrounding our business.

Borderless Business and Career: The Secret to Building Winning Global Teams

It didn't take me long to realize there were more borders to be broken. That's one of the beautiful things about this process: there are always more borders to break, but with each new freedom you achieve, your capability to identify and overcome the next border grows exponentially.

As a tech entrepreneur in New York City, the need was great, but our reach was limited. Technology doesn't sleep. Clients, especially our Wall Street customers, needed constant monitoring of their computer networks because even the briefest service interruption could result in millions of dollars lost. When it comes to stocks, milliseconds count.

The demands were clear: Our clients required nothing short of 24/7 help desk support and flawless technology management. Yet, I could only provide services between 8 a.m. and 5 p.m.. I looked to expand these hours but found myself boxed in again when I couldn't find tech talent willing to work at night or on weekends.

The solution to this border came to me when I least expected it. I was working out at the Equinox gym, nestled within the iconic Grand Central Station, and I read an article in *The New York Times* about how tech titans like Microsoft and Google resolved their 24/7 help desk issues by leveraging global talent from different time zones.

If they weren't letting the literal border of the country stop them, neither would I. What's more, I realized my Indian roots—the same situation that had caused borders earlier in my life—would now give me an unfair advantage. I was well-versed in the cultures of both India and the U.S., leaving me perfectly positioned to find the right connections and hires in both countries.

I built my own training division to meet the service standards of the U.S., including areas like culture integration and alignment, accent neutralization, and tech skills. These processes broke all the traditional borders of delivering service 24/7 and eliminated any doubts associated with providing quality, reputable, secure service.

Our winning global teams became our competitive edge and fueled more growth for the business. Using the capability we had built, we started doubling down on collaborations. My business peers (tech competitors) saw something unique happening: almost overnight, my business was growing exponentially faster than theirs. Everyone wanted to know how we were surpassing the wave of growth and profit the rest of the industry was riding.

Because most of our competitors lacked the multicultural experience to build 24/7 help desks on their own, they collaborated with us. We added so much value to these relationships that they became our champions. Breaking the global talent border solved our own difficulties with scalability and added the unforeseen possibilities of unlimited expansion in the realm of collaboration as well.[1]

Born Borderless

Every life can be defined by its borders. But the most magnetic people are those who define themselves by the borders they've broken.

I first saw the Statue of Liberty as an immigrant who had just risked it all in an effort to start again. Little did I know my journey would come full circle. When I arrived in the U.S., I didn't even have twelve dollars to buy a ferry ticket to Liberty Island.

Twenty-eight years later, we made history by renting out the entire island to host an annual conference (the first-ever MSP tech conference) for our clients. I don't know of a better way to demonstrate the power of a Borderless Life. Foreign land had become Freedom land.

Do you have a Liberty Island dream? What iconic moment would represent a life with no borders for you? Whatever your Liberty Island moment looks like, it will require identifying and breaking your borders.

As we dive into the specifics of what a Borderless Life can look like for you, I will make you two promises. First, it will be a tough journey. Borders are just adversity. You cannot go above or below them; you have to go through them. There are no shortcuts. "Bordered" is not synonymous with "bad" or "painful" or even "undesirable." There are not always clear indicators or pain points to signify that your life is not all that it could be.

When I was working as a tech professional, it would have been easy to content myself with that life. But I was holding myself back from having the Liberty Island moment I'd dreamed about.

My second promise to you is that a Borderless Life is worth the discomfort and uncertainty. Although we all have borders imposed on us soon after we're born, we are born borderless. When you actualize a Borderless Life for yourself, you are fulfilling your life as it should be. Your reach will be infinite, your abundance will be limitless, and your impact will stretch to the outer reaches of human possibility.

2

The Mindsets of Borderless Life

Learning the What, Why, and How

I recently undertook a momentous item on my bucket list: hiking to Mount Everest Base Camp. My son and I spent seven days trekking through rugged terrain, scaling peaks, and learning to thrive without essentials like electricity and clean water, which I often take for granted.

Reaching Everest Base Camp was a moment I'll never forget. Standing there at 17,598 feet above sea level, I was overwhelmed by the joy of sharing such an accomplishment with my son. It was a culmination of another border broken, and Everest itself rising above us was a beautiful depiction of what a Borderless Life can look like.

What heights could you climb to if nothing held you back?

As I reflected on my journey, which was partially in celebration of my fiftieth birthday, I realized there are no less than fifty fundamental lessons I could name as takeaways from the trip. All of them are essential to living a Borderless Life. As we continue to explore the next steps in breaking borders, I will share these lessons where applicable. You can find a complete list of these lessons at the end of the book.

Borderless Lessons from Everest #1

Every mountain has ten peaks inside it.

The route to Everest is not straightforward. In order to reach Everest's peak, you have to go over ten other peaks first. You hike up and down full mountains ten times before you've reached your primary objective.

The journey toward Borderless Life is the same. You will have many necessary ups and downs, but as long as you are heading toward your goal, you're on the right track. Don't worry when you're going down because another mountain is ahead, ready for you to start your ascent again. And your Everest is always in the distance—Borderless Life rising endlessly into the sky.

Having something to keep you steady through the ups and downs of your journey is essential. I've discovered Three Mindsets of Borderless Life that will keep you steady if you commit to them throughout your journey.

The Three Mindsets of Borderless Life

No matter what border you are facing, there are three mind-sets you must commit to. Think of these as the what, the why, and the how of Borderless Life. First, we must know what we are pursuing.

What is Borderless Life? Ultimately, it is a mentality. When we expand our vision to see life as a series of restrictions and containments we have to overcome, the steps to reach that vision become clearer.

For that reason, the first mindset is Think Borderless. Before taking any action, we have to cultivate a mindset that expands our vision rather than restricts it. Learn to look at your life as a series of possibilities. What is preventing those possibilities from becoming reality? Are these borders self-imposed?

Imagine for a moment that you wanted to ascend to Everest Base Camp. You're going to run into immediate difficulties, whether they be financial, physical, logistical, or any of a thousand others.

Maybe you start telling yourself, "That's a silly idea, I could never do it," or "It's too hard." Your self-talk could even be something as simple as "It's not worth the effort" or "I don't want to do it that badly." These are all self-imposed borders. The sooner you recognize them as such, the easier it will be to break through them all and reach your Everest.

When you have a Borderless Thinking mentality, you're always looking for these thought patterns that hold you back. Think beyond what you're thinking today.

The second mindset focuses on the "why" of Borderless Life. What motivates you to continue seeking an ever-expanding life even when it gets difficult? One of my greatest motivations when I left my birthplace behind for foreign lands was the assurance that my impact and ability to help others would grow each time I broke the border of my capability. For that reason, the second mindset is Grow Your Reach.

As a farmer in India, I could have served my village and the surrounding community by producing and selling goods, but my reach would have been severely limited by my geographical borders. Because I broke that border, I extended my reach and my impact. Now, the world is my marketplace. As a tech entrepreneur, I have a global delivery center that can deliver around the clock, following the sun, and serving any market at any time.

When you know who you want to impact, you have your reason for breaking borders. This will propel you through every difficulty and doubt on your journey.

Finally, we must know *how* to achieve a Borderless Life. In the next few chapters, we'll explore many practical avenues for breaking borders, but the number one strategy is to always be growing. In other words, Become a Lifelong Learner, which is our third mindset. When you are constantly learning and growing, you are always moving past intellectual borders. Those borders will never stop, so the best way to combat them is to never stop learning to break them.

Lifelong Learning requires resilience because as those borders continue, it will feel like the ten mountains we climb on our way to Everest. The constant ups and downs are exhausting. But resilience involves overcoming those challenges with grace, both for yourself and for others.

Each time we feel like we're failing, the Borderless Thinking mindset will help you realize you're only going down a mountain, and the Lifelong Learning mindset will help you learn from the experience so you're better prepared for the next.

If you make sure you're living by these three mindsets, you've already taken the first step toward a Borderless Life. You know your what, why, and how. These will all work together to create value and perspective for you as you're searching out borders in your life and discovering ways to break them open.

PART 2

Breaking Borders

3

The Car of Needs

What Gets Me Where I Want to Go?

You are probably familiar with Maslow's Hierarchy of Needs. It's a simple depiction of the types of requirements a person needs fulfilled in order to live. Abraham Maslow proposed this model in the 1940s, and it quickly gained popularity as a way to understand human behavior.[2]

However, this framework lacks one all-important feature: direction. Viewing life's needs as static removes the driving force for life. In light of this insight, I created a new framework: the Car of Needs.

If you're driving a car, we can assume a couple of things:

1. You're going somewhere. Even if you don't have a destination in mind, the act of driving is going to take you from one location to another. Of course, if

you know where you are going and the main highway to get there, you'll have a clear vision, and you'll know your center. If you take a wrong exit, you will have a strong enough sense of your center (main highway) to make a U-turn and get back on track.

2. You have the necessary machinery to move along. A car needs four wheels in order to move. If your car is missing a wheel, it's probably not going anywhere, at least not easily.

Why do these assumptions make a car a good model for life? Like a car, your life is going somewhere. You are always moving towards a new destination, even if you don't know what that destination is. Your purpose, vision, values, and mindset determine which way you steer, although some people are more intentional with these than others. We'll talk later about planning your destination, but for now, just know that direction is an important aspect of your life.

A car is also like life in that you need certain "machinery" in order to move forward. For a car, it's tires. For life, it's these four elements:

- Health
- Relationships
- Career
- Impact

A successful life must have a "wheel" that corresponds to each of these areas. These will look different for everyone, and some people will have more in some areas than others. But there is one equality we are all born with: we all have 168 hours in a week. The most basic resource—time—is always the same across the board.

I always talk about these 168 hours as PSI—the measure of air pressure in your tires. If we divide 168 by 4, we get 42 PSI per tire, so a perfectly equal division of time into our four aspects of life results in 42 hours to spend each week. I represent this with the Car of Needs diagram:

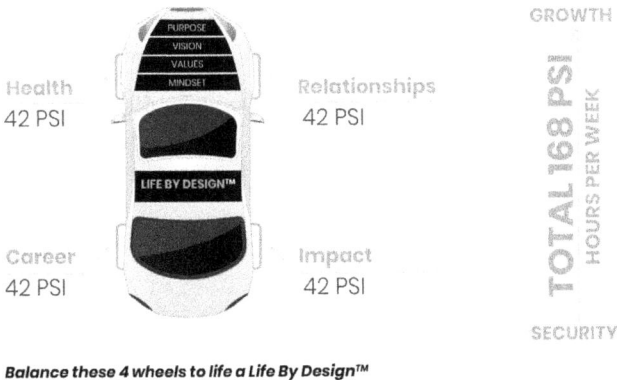

Balance these 4 wheels to life a Life By Design™

The other way your total PSI affects your car is in the basic physiological need for security. Before anything else, we must fulfill our basic survival instinct. If we do not feel safe and secure, or if we feel like we are in imminent danger, everything else drops off our radar.

All of our hours go toward gaining security first if we do not already have it. The problem here is that survival mode is static. You can never grow when every hour is spent trying to survive.

On the right side of the diagram, you'll see the hours per week scale. Security is at the bottom because it is such a basic need. But as you gain security, you free up your hours to spend on other things. You're moving up the growth scale.

Where do you invest your hours as you free them up? You put the PSI in the Four Wheels of Life.

The Four Wheels of Life

The Four Wheels of Life are health, relationships, career, and impact. Everything necessary for a fulfilling life is included in these areas. The diagram above shows a perfectly balanced life: 42 PSI allotted to each wheel. Perfect balance is impossible, though. So instead, we seek harmony. The wheels don't need to have equal pressure, but they do need harmony with each other.

Perhaps in your twenties, career and relationships both have 50 or 60 PSI as you establish yourself professionally and invest in a future spouse. In the next decade, you might start to realize that the health of youth is not everlasting, so you start to spend more time on intentional wellness practices. Perhaps in your fifties, you are spending less time on your career, but you have started to consider the legacy of your life, so you invest in community service. Your impact PSI would then be proportionally higher.

Different personalities, circumstances, and phases of life will influence the allocation of PSI. What is important to remember, though, is you must have a base level in all four tires in order to keep moving.

What happens when you get a flat tire? Your car starts veering to one side, taking you off course. If you try to ignore the problem and keep driving, you not only have to overcorrect your steering to compensate for the loss, but you also risk causing costly damage to the car.

When you lose too much pressure in a Wheel of Life, you will veer off course. Whatever goal you have for your life is no longer straight ahead. For example, if you're hoping to live wealthily after retirement, you might be tempted to throw everything into your career. Your PSI in career might increase to sixty, seventy, or eighty, but those hours don't appear out of thin air. You must take them from another wheel.

If you take too many hours from your health, you will not be well enough to enjoy your retirement if you live that long in the first place.

If you take them instead from relationships, you will not have friends or companionship in your later years because you didn't invest the time in other people when you were younger.

And if you instead take the extra out of impact, your life, no matter how comfortable it is, will lack any meaning. You will not have positively affected the world when you leave it.

Harmony is essential.

Borderless Lessons from Everest #2, #3, and #4

You carry capability, not comfort.

When you decide to climb to Everest Base Camp, comfort is the last thing you should expect to find on the journey. It's not an easy journey, but if it were, there would be no point in starting up the mountain in the first place.

Comfort is not the goal—clarity is.

Life works the same way. Don't set comfort as your goal, especially when you're attempting to find harmony in the Four Wheels of Life. It might be easy to focus only on your Career so you can live comfortably, but you will be missing out on the joys and rewards of Relationships, Health, and Impact.

The climb reveals what comfort conceals.

As you choose to step away from comfort to pursue loftier goals, you will start to identify what means the most to you.

Borderless Horizons

You may be wondering what the Car of Needs has to do with borders. *Sure, there are four needs we have to fulfill in order to get anywhere in life, but how do I achieve an ever-expanding future?* That's the big question.

In short, the Car of Needs provides a comprehensive model of life so we can systematically begin identifying and breaking borders. Knowing that something is holding you back is not helpful unless you know what it is and which area of life it originates in. So by using the Four Wheels of Life as a guide, we can locate different borders and implement strategies to break them.

Each person requires a unique harmony of PSI in their wheels to achieve an optimal speed. Breaking borders is like identifying the perfect amount of time to allot to each Wheel of Life so that your future is an open road, expanding into the endless horizon.

4

Borderless Health

Achieving Holistic Abundance of Mind, Body, and Soul

I recently celebrated my fiftieth birthday, which, for many people, tends to be a dreaded milestone. Reaching fifty years old can feel like you're "over the hill" or in a constant decline. My experience has been just the opposite.

Based on my biomarkers and different tests I've done, my biological age is ten years younger than my chronological age. This means I can celebrate my birthday without the fear of old age because so many more factors determine my health than just the number of years I've been alive.

Viewing age as anything more than a number is a limiting border, and escaping it has freed me to live life happily and healthily.

Common Borders in Health

You may be generally aware that your health is something to be taken care of, but unseen borders might be holding you back from taking a proactive approach to caring for your mind, body, and spirit in a way that promotes abundance.

The most common health border is a limiting mindset about health. Do you have a health-first mindset? Are you cultivating daily habits that promote well-being? I always say that if you're not living your Life by Design, you're living by default.

Unfortunately, the default when it comes to wellness, whether it's physical, mental, or spiritual, is a steady decline in health. Age tends to make us weaker and more prone to illness and disease. This is a border on its own, but just trying to fight aging ignores the root of the problem: mindset.

If you have not been guided by health-first thinking your whole life, then, naturally, age is going to become a serious problem. On the other hand, if you've been intentional in establishing healthy habits your whole life, age will not affect you as severely.

Borderless Lessons from Everest #5 and #6

Commitment is day one. Consistency is day one hundred.

It's easy to say, "I'm going to climb to Everest Base Camp." It's not as easy to follow through when you're actually on the trail. Thinking long-term is key to establishing consistency in endeavors like ascending mountains and maintaining health into your old age. As you commit to healthy practices now, remember that you will reap the benefits of your consistency years down the road.

You train for Everest long before Base Camp.

Every workout, every run, every challenge I took on before Everest was preparing me for that climb, even though I wasn't deliberately training for it yet. In the same way, every small effort you make toward your health now is preparation for your future, even if you don't see immediate benefits.

Almost every other border can be traced back to this one. If you're struggling with your health in any respect and you don't know where to start, try examining your health mindset. Ask yourself:

- Do I consider my health when making daily decisions?

- Do I have habits intended to build my wellness?

- When do I sacrifice health in order to achieve less important goals?

Another common border is the lack of discipline. This can manifest as a broad issue, like jumping between various health trends without spending enough time on any of them to start seeing results. It also could be a specific issue, like not drinking enough water, not having a daily workout routine, or consistently allowing stress to affect your behavior. A discipline border is not due to a lack of knowledge but a lack of commitment.

External influences and communities also present borders. If you are not part of a healthy community or are surrounded by people who are not health-focused, it can be even more challenging to maintain healthy habits.

For example, if your family brings unhealthy food into the house, you may be consistently tempted to partake in less-than-ideal meals. It's important to remember, however, that you always have agency, even in these circumstances. Blaming others for unhealthy choices is an example of a Bordered Mindset.

Furthermore, keeping negative people in your life is a direct barrier to health. Regardless of other healthy practices, negative people can make you unhealthy physically, mentally, and in every other way.

Finally, procrastination and a lack of organization in addressing health issues can be major borders. Perhaps you have trouble keeping track of your health needs, or maybe you have a habit of delaying necessary medical appointments and not taking action on blood work results.

You can achieve borderless health by paying attention to these general borders, but it is also helpful to take a closer look at three aspects of health: mind, body, and spirit. Investigating these in your own life can help you realize what has been holding you back without you even knowing it.

Mind

As I've already mentioned, health is determined to a large degree by your mindset. When your thinking is borderless, your life will be borderless. So, maintaining positive and constructive thoughts will work wonders in breaking down barriers.

The most important advice I can give for your health in general is to prioritize mental health. We all have responsibilities and pressures pulling us in a million directions, but you have to put your own oxygen mask on first before you can help your child put theirs on.

Your priorities might be misplaced if you find yourself believing you must be there for family, kids, or others without recognizing that you must first be healthy yourself to be helpful or useful. Investing in yourself is not being selfish when it comes to mental health. You have to be in good mental health before you can invest in others.

A large part of maintaining mental health is self-assurance. If you let others consistently influence your choices, you will lack the consistency and security to remain grounded in any situation.

I'm not saying other people should never influence you. I am always reading books, listening to podcasts, and allowing myself to learn from the experience and expertise of those around me.

But be aware: There are so many opinions out there. Protect yourself from faulty information, being overwhelmed, and fleeting trends by assessing what you learn and only applying the things that lead toward a Borderless Life.

When you learn about a new mental health practice or are tempted to start a new habit, first ask yourself: Will this expand my capabilities and reach, or limit them?

If you even find that something is limiting you by stealing time or resources, cut it out of your life. Some habits might be objectively beneficial, but if they are not helping you to live with less stress, then they are borders. This applies to people as well. Surrounding yourself with growth-mindset, positive-focused people will do wonders for boosting your mental health.

Borderless Lessons from Everest #7 and #8

Climbing is a mindset, not a trail.

The most transformational part of the ascent to Everest Base Camp is not the physical act of climbing. It is how your mindset climbs to higher perspectives during the ascent. During the difficult, dangerous circumstances, are you letting your mind wander to fears and uncertainties, or are you focusing on the determination and grit you will need to make it through? This climbing mindset is essential for everyday life as we face mental borders.

Mind follows altitude. So does emotion.

What is your mental altitude? How high have you climbed on your own personal Everest journey to overcome harmful thought patterns and expand your vision and reach?

Body

When I was thirty, I didn't care much about health—physical, mental, or spiritual. It's that age where you don't care if you get enough sleep, you're overworked, and you don't give any thought to reading, working out, or nutrition. And just like any other tech professional or tech entrepreneur, I had a tech tummy from eating poorly and sitting at my desk all day without much exercise.

I realized the border that my health habits were creating around my lifespan, so I soon made changes in my habits. I started to sleep more, eat healthier foods, and exercise regularly. I focused on having a disciplined morning routine every day.

I also decided to take a three-month break from drinking at the beginning of each year. It helped me start my year with discipline. I started that about ten years ago, but in 2020 when so many people were confined to their homes, I started to see stories in the news about all these people who were struggling with drinking problems more than usual because they were day drinking or just sitting around at home.

That year, I decided to extend my commitment to no alcohol for the whole year. I continued through April and all the way through December. As the year progressed, I noticed some changes in my health. I started feeling better than I ever had. I was overeating less because my body didn't have to cope with the alcohol anymore. I was even sleeping more regularly, and my sleep score was higher than ever.

It was easier to wake up in the morning, exercise, and follow through with my routine. It was like I was on a well-being high, and I realized there was no sense in going back to my old habits of having a glass of wine in the evening if I could feel this good all the time without it. I continued for the next few years and saw my health only expand.

The other crucial benefit I received from this yearly practice was the assurance that I had the willpower to control my health choices with absoluteness. If I recognize a different issue with my habits, whether it's eating too many chocolate chip cookies or a tendency to slouch or a lack of exercise, I know with certainty that I have the willpower to change.

Anytime you choose to say no to something for a significant amount of time, you build resilience. That resilience then helps you grow and adapt continuously as you pursue Borderless Health!

This story illustrates two of the crucial aspects of bodily health: observation and assessment. When it comes to physical wellness, make sure you are objectively assessing how you feel and what actually makes a difference in how you operate. If you are not aware of issues or solutions, your health is limited by a border.

When you do know what parts of your physical health need help, consider starting a Fix List. You might have one of these for your car or your house. Something breaks, but it's not absolutely urgent, so you put it on a list and wait until the next time you're ready to take the car into the shop.

The strategy works just as well for your body. When something needs "fixed" eventually, it's easy to forget about it for weeks, months, and even years as life carries on as normal. The problem is that the issue can get worse the longer you leave it alone.

One of my teeth was giving me some trouble years ago, but I didn't go get it looked at immediately. I procrastinated and let a whole decade go by. It turns out the tooth actually caused me to lose a lot of the bone in my jaw, and I needed to have a bridge put in to fix the problem.

If I had gotten the tooth fixed right away, or at least in a timely manner, I would have saved myself a lot of pain and trouble. Keeping a Fix List now helps me keep track of health issues and address them before they become an even greater problem.

Similarly, blood work results usually provide a pretty clear picture of what we need to change in order to stay healthy, but do we take action on it? It should go on your Fix List, and as you check on your Fix List regularly, you can schedule the necessary appointments to keep you moving toward Borderless Health.

Maybe you need braces, or your blood sugar is high, or you have trouble sleeping. Whenever something is not quite right, put it on your Fix List. These can become borders to your health if you do not take action early.

Borderless Lessons from Everest #9

Stillness reveals the next move.

Sometimes when you see obstacles ahead, you aren't sure what your next move should be. I experienced this while climbing to Everest Base Camp. Maybe your footing is unsure or the path is hidden. I found that stillness—taking time to calmly assess the situation—reveals many answers.

This is why it is so important to take time to observe and assess health issues. You might not know the next move forward with your health until you take the time to be still and let the answers reveal themselves.

Soul

If mind refers to mental health and body refers to physical health, then soul refers to your spiritual health. Spirituality can mean many different things to different people, but no matter what your beliefs are, you have spiritual health that must be cared for in order to live borderless.

The first border to overcome is apathy toward your own soul. Do you recognize your soul as a part of you that must be fed and kept in good health? Do you acknowledge there are powers beyond human understanding and imagination? Are there practices you consistently engage in, such as meditation, prayer, or contemplation, that promote spiritual wellness?

Overcoming soul-related borders involves recognizing the importance of inner peace, spirituality, and beliefs for your overall well-being and actively caring about feeding your soul.

Borderless Lessons from Everest #10

You don't conquer Everest. You align with it.

Everest is a force of nature. Some people claim to "conquer" Everest when they finish their journey, but the real victory comes from aligning yourself with the mountain. The soul is like Everest in this respect. When you overcome soul boundaries, you do not do so by conquering. Instead, you become more aligned with your soul and the forces of nature that influence it.

Best Practices for Borderless Health

I've shared a few strategies for breaking borders surrounding your health, but I'll summarize those and add a few more that may be helpful as you begin your journey.

- **Keep a Fix List.** I shared this in the context of physical health, but it is helpful for mental and spiritual health as well. Every time you recognize that something is not right, add it to the list. That way, even if you don't have the time or resources to address the issue immediately, you have a record and reminder to take care of yourself in specific ways.

- **Sunny's Sunrise Routine.** I mentioned briefly that I follow a strict morning routine. I wake up at 4 a.m., exercise, meditate, and sit down for coffee with my wife before beginning work. Even on days I don't have a lot of time, I sit down for at least a sip of coffee, and my wife and I tell each other, "I'm grateful for you." Even such a simple practice can be life-changing as you begin your day with gratitude and a positive mindset. What will your Sunrise Routine be?

- **Three-Two-One Rule.** I use this rule for better sleep. Three hours before your bedtime should be your last meal. Two hours before your bedtime, you should stop drinking water. One hour before your bedtime, you should stop using any screens or phones. This works wonders for your sleep quality and overall restfulness. Then, try not to use your phone during your Sunrise Routine either, just to make sure you limit external stressors and influences while you prepare for the day.

- **Health Walk.** I go for a walk every weekend with ten to twelve friends. Yes, walking is good for my physical health, but spending this time with similarly-minded friends helps to boost my mental health as well. We get to talk, laugh together, and unwind from the week. Consider implementing a Health Walk into your schedule with friends who will build you up.

5

Borderless Relationships

Seeking Authenticity in Social Life

I was once asked if there was one thing everyone should do in order to have Borderless Relationships. There's an easy answer: travel! Make friends all over the world, and borders will never hold you back. On a more serious note, relationships over international borders are certainly beneficial, but literal borders are not the only ones to consider when striving for your ever-expanding future.

There are all sorts of emotional and mental barriers when it comes to relationships, but these are some of the most important barriers to overcome. Relationships are the most important part of a Borderless Life. Why? Because no matter how wealthy you are, no matter how long you live, no matter how successful you are in any sense of the word, you will never be truly fulfilled if you don't have healthy relationships. The deepest joys of life come from connections between people.

There is so much suffering in the world. When people say that, they often refer to physical pain and hardship—starvation, poverty, and other brutal realities of life. I don't mean to make light of this type of suffering, but consider that this is not the only type of suffering I see. When I meet some people, they might be billionaires with everything they could possibly want, but if they don't have authentic relationships, they suffer, too.

All the other Wheels of Life are by-products of this wheel. For example, you will never be able to have good health if you are not surrounded with wholesome people. They will impact your well-being. A lot of people will get into bad eating, drinking, or sleeping habits because they are in so much pain due to their relationships, both personal and professional. Relationships can be energy builders or energy disruptors in our lives. The healthier your relationships, the healthier your mind, body, and soul will be.

Borderless Lessons from Everest #11

Every step either elevates or exhausts.

The climb is always taking you somewhere, but you must always be cautious about where each step is leading you. On Everest, each step must have the purpose of elevating you. In relationships, each person you interact with must elevate both parties. Otherwise, that relationship will simply exhaust you, leaving you little energy to invest in others.

How can you achieve Borderless Relationships? Once again, it comes down to a mindset. Are you placing appropriate emphasis on the quality of your relationships? Have you recently assessed which of your relationships are building you up and which are tearing you down?

I encourage you to establish a regular rhythm for answering this question. It could be quarterly or annual but set aside time to perform a Relationship Audit for your life. Answer the questions:

- What are my top relationships? Who do I spend the most time with?

- Which of these relationships are healthy?

- Which are unhealthy?

Once you've assessed, you'll know what good and bad look like in your relationships, and you can start to form a plan for action. Perform this audit for all three types of relationships: family, friends, and professional collaborators.

Family and Friends

Family and friends make up the most important relationships, and they create the most rewarding moments of your life. But no relationship is free from difficulty, and at some point, your family and friends will be on the wrong side of your Relationship Audit. You can't choose your family like you can your friends, but dealing with both comes down to the same key principles.

Where possible, it's better to fix a relationship rather than cut it off completely. Try to identify the pain points. Articulate your feelings and the problem to the other person.

How do you expect them to change? Is there a way you can change? Is the other person naysaying you? Is there a misalignment of values or motivations?

If you have been transparent, diligently seeking a solution to the problem, and the other person does nothing, then you may not be able to fix that relationship. You cannot change the other person, but you can change how you think about the relationship. Be courageous in your decision to love them the way they are, but don't invite them into your day-to-day life in a way that affects your health, career, or impact negatively.

I had a few close friends during my high school and college years who are no longer friends. It isn't because we gradually grew apart, but because I had to intentionally close the door on those relationships in order to continue towards my Borderless Life.

Another friend and I were so close that we started a business together, but this person began taking advantage of me and my kindness. While I was trying to be helpful, my friend saw my behavior as something to manipulate. I had to assess the situation and say no to having the person in my life anymore.

The hardest situations are when a relative is unwilling to listen or change. It's very difficult for me to give up on family structure, but sometimes it is necessary. I had a relative who never had a positive outlook. He was very helpful to me growing up, but it got to the point where I did not want to be around him because of how he affected me. It was very difficult to communicate that I would not be interacting with him much anymore.

Now, however, I catch up with him every now and again, and he has told me that he understands now why I stepped back from the relationship for a while. It took many years, but we have been able to start on the journey of repairing our relationship because I took the time to make sure he knew I still respected and loved him.

The key through all of these situations is to set your expectations, define the guidelines you live by, and know your values. Hold firmly to your values, no matter what, and when there is conflict, make sure people know what those values are and why they are important to you. If people know how you communicate and why you act the way you do, the relationship will be infinitely stronger.

The other benefit of maintaining your values with strength is that while you can be kind and giving, people will not mistake your kindness for weakness. Standing up for yourself in the face of injustice does not negate your kindness or amiability. It protects you from being in a situation where you can no longer be genuine because people have taken advantage of you.

This is very important because, a lot of times, the people who have a reputation for being very helpful and generous don't want to communicate clearly in the midst of a conflict for fear of offending someone. If you communicate clearly and confidently, people around you will know you cannot be taken for a ride. You might be the kindest person they have ever met, but that does not mean anyone can walk all over you.

Even when you have healthy relationships, you still need to ensure your rules and boundaries are clearly defined so that there is no margin for any unhealthy behavior to creep in. If you invest proper time and attention in them, there is less chance of those relationships becoming unhealthy.

Professional Collaboration

In the early days of my tech business, we had a moment where three out of four of our employees left us due to a bad experience, and my wife and I had to reassess our approach to professional relationships. We identified Three Relationship-First Strategies to use in order to create a healthy environment.

First, we had to attract the right people. Most friction in a relationship—either personal or professional—comes from misaligned values. The atmosphere of our company completely changed when we hired people aligned with our values and vision.

Second, we built a people-first culture. We prioritized relationships over revenue. We cultivated trust and open communication and focused on adding real value to team members in terms of overall growth and well-being.

Third, we emphasized collaborative teamwork. Effective collaboration requires an intense focus on individual strengths, leveraged together to drive success. We encouraged roles that maximize each team member's unique talents.

Simply by focusing on relationships first, we turned our company into a place where people love to work, and as a side effect, our company grew in profitability and impact as well.

The average person spends half of their life at work. This is a fantastic statistic if your job is aligned with your passion, but it's somewhat unfortunate if not. Regardless, this means for half of your life, you will be surrounded by professional relationships.

If you happen to be in a managerial position, you have some control over who you work with. You have the power to hire or fire people who are difficult to work with. If you don't have this level of control, you have to take a different approach.

The only way to choose your team members is to leave or join a company. If you have to leave a position due to relationships, you might consider starting your own company. Entrepreneurship puts you in a position of freedom to pick and choose only team members who can cultivate healthy relationships.

Remember: People don't leave companies; they leave bad relationships. So, you either have to be in a position where you can choose who to work with, or you must know very clearly when it's time for you to leave a company because it will negatively impact your whole life if you are spending half your time in poor relationships.

Borderless Lessons from Everest #12 and #13

You don't rise alone—teams elevate together.

If you attempt something as momentous as climbing to Everest Base Camp, you must be conscious of who is on your team. Your team will go everywhere with you and share in every win and loss.

One slow teammate sets the pace.

Whoever is the slowest will always set the pace. The same is true in any professional situation. Whoever is the least efficient on your team will determine your maximum capacity. Be aware of who you surround yourself with at all times, and look for ways to help those teammates.

Best Practices for Borderless Relationships

There are seven billion people in the world. I can't personally add value to seven billion lives. I have to pick and choose. I meet so many wonderful people at airports, train stations, and conferences, and I wish them all the best, but you can only choose some relationships. Human capacity is in the 250 to 280 range for people you can actually be close with. Beyond that, the human brain capacity is not designed to serve those relationships. So we all must choose who we want to contribute to. We hope that those we choose will contribute to us, too.

Here are some strategies to use as you start to seek Borderless Relationships:

- Perform your Relationship Audit yearly at the least. Feel free to do it more often if necessary, especially if you are constantly meeting and spending time with new people. Form your two lists—healthy relation-ships and unhealthy relationships—and create a plan for maintaining the healthy ones and fixing or giving up the unhealthy ones.

- Build your company (or assess the company you work for) with a Relationship-First mentality. Use the three steps to build a stronger culture and a more profitable business model.

6

Borderless Career

Defying Professional Limits and Pursuing Purpose

T here is a good reason career is one of the Four Wheels of Life: money is a necessity, whether we like it or not. Often, money can become a border as people do not have enough to get where they want to go, or they get stuck in a "just a little bit more" mindset. The pursuit of money becomes the main driving force rather than a means to a Borderless Life. Your career can also become a border if it starts to limit your opportunities instead of broadening them. But as with everything we have discussed so far, it starts with a mindset change.

There are only two things that will make money in your life. One is your skill. We are hired and advance in our industry because of particular skill sets, from general capabilities like critical thinking or communication to technical abilities like coding or piloting. When your skill increases, your paycheck will increase as well. This is a fact of life, although it can feel contrary to reality at times. The truth is, if there is any imbalance between your skill level and your paycheck, it will be temporary.

This works both ways. If you are being paid more than your skill or effort warrants, people will eventually notice and fire you if you are an employee, or they will stop investing in your company as a client or consumer if you are an entrepreneur.

On the flip side, if your paycheck is less than what your skill deserves, people will acknowledge that imbalance, and you will get a raise or be promoted. If this doesn't happen, you can quit and start at a new position or company that does value your skill properly.

Everything will remain in balance in the long run. What this means is if you're trying to break a professional or financial border, one of the ways to proceed is to increase your skill.

This might sound like an impractical and idealistic solution, but increasing your skill does not necessarily require hundreds of hours of concentrated effort. It can, especially if you are working to develop a highly technical skill, but we've already discussed how skill comes in many forms. Increasing your value in the workplace can be as simple as developing the mindset of a lifelong learner.

Intellectual Career

Too often, we tend to limit intellectual growth to formal education. While formal education is important, be careful not to limit your education to the years spent in high school or college.

Remember the third Mindset of Borderless Life? It's Lifelong Learning. That means that no matter where you are in life or how far removed you are from your college education, you should always be expanding your intellect.

Learning comes in many forms. Maybe you are improving a skill set in order to advance in your career, or maybe you're simply studying a subject that interests you with no concrete agenda in mind. I love to read new books and listen to podcasts to increase my knowledge, but that does not mean everything I learn is immediately applicable to my life. Instead, every time I learn something new, I am exercising my intellect so that I am always expanding my capacity.

If you become a lifelong learner, you will continue to grow throughout your life, and the capacity will open doors in your career as you make yourself more valuable. The next time you start to feel stuck at work, take a moment to consider what the border in front of you really is.

First, have you been diligent in increasing your learning and skill in consistent, manageable ways? Have you set yourself up for a successful borderless career? If your intellectual trajectory is moving upwards and outwards, then the issue lies somewhere else.

Are you feeling undervalued based on your skill and effort? If so, you have two options. Have patience, and everything will balance out eventually. Alternatively, take a leap of faith and leave, remembering that you are leaving a bad relationship rather than a bad company.

Another question to ask yourself when you're feeling stuck in a professional capacity is whether you have a passion for your work. Your work might be creating a border for you because it is draining your energy rather than replenishing it.

This doesn't mean you should work less to preserve your energy, but it might mean you should pivot your direction toward something you feel strongly about. I am often busier than ever as I travel, speak, and oversee a million different things at once, but even then, I am full of energy because I am so passionate about what I do.

When you do something with passion, then no matter what is going on in your life, you will feel energy. Find the things that give you energy and the borders will start to fall away as your joy propels you forward.

Borderless Lessons from Everest #14

Lifelong Learning makes every step lighter.

I loved climbing to Everest Base Camp. Was it difficult and painful? Yes. But I gained so much value because my focus was on Lifelong Learning. These Lessons from Everest are the manifestation of that mindset. I was always looking for new ways to expand my knowledge and wisdom, even while I was climbing mountains.

No matter how heavy your burdens seem at the moment, a Lifelong Learning mindset can make them lighter.

Investment

Skill is the first thing that makes money. We've seen how you have some degree of control over your skill level, but there is another border preventing an unlimited increase in your paycheck due to skill.

Skill has a limitation of forty hours per week. Sure, you might decide to allot more of your 168 hours per week to your professional development, but doing so for too long will destroy the harmony between your Four Wheels of Life. If you consistently spend sixty to eighty hours per week on your career, then your health, relationships, and impact will start to suffer in no time at all.

Therefore, in order to break the financial borders that skill limitations place on us, we have to turn to the other thing that makes money: money. Your money will make more money when you manage it properly, and it does not require the same time investment as your job.

I bought my first house in Jersey City right after college, but I didn't have any money. How did I do it? I got a credit card with an offer of zero interest for the first year, and I borrowed money from friends to make the down payment. I then began to rent out part of the house while I was paying for it, and I bought more real estate. I made my money make more money.

There are many ways to invest, but whatever you decide to do, make the formula work for you: make your money make more money. Investing is always a calculated risk. To me, real estate is the most reliable way to do this, but consider it for yourself with whatever means are available to you.

The best advice I can give you from a career and financial standpoint is to know your means and live within them. Don't allow what you see on social media or in someone else's life to influence your behavior if you are not in the same circumstances as them. Rather, be honest with yourself about your resources and live a practical life. You can still be growing exponentially, but only if you don't exceed your means by thinking you should be somewhere you're not.

It all comes back to the Car of Needs. Someone else's car might be far down the road, but just because they are further along than you does not mean you should live like them. You might not even be headed to the same destination!

Live by design where you are, and seek your own goals rather than the goals of others.

Borderless Lessons from Everest #15, #16, #17, #18, and #19

If you're not elevating, you're not progressing.

There are so many lessons I learned from Everest that can be put in investment terms because any achievement follows the same pattern of putting money or effort in and reaping the rewards. Every investment I made in Everest took me higher up. If you aren't investing in something that will grow, you are wasting your resources.

Slow is smooth. Smooth is fast.

Climbing Everest is not a sprint. In the same way, investment does not happen quickly. It requires slowness of deliberation and the smoothness of a plan.

Courage starts the climb. Grit finishes it.

Investment requires risk. Be smart about your risk, but have the courage to take a step of faith, knowing that your grit and determination will help see that risk through to a reward.

Walking flat means walking in circles.

If your investments or career are taking you in circles, maybe you need to reassess your elevation. Are you constantly seeking out the next mountain to climb?

Your next step must be higher.

It doesn't matter what your next step looks like as long as it is higher than the one before. Seek bolder investments, find new career opportunities, but whatever you do, go higher!

Best Practices for Borderless Career

- Become a Lifelong Learner. The best way to increase your skill in the long term is to do it little by little. Find some way to increase your intellectual capacity every day.

- Remember that any imbalance between skill and paycheck is only temporary.

- Make sure your passion is driving your career. When you are passionate about something, you will have energy no matter what else is going on in your life.

7

Borderless Impact

Embracing the World as Your Marketplace

Some aspects of life are only for you. We all want borderless careers, health, and relationships in order to live a better life, but if you step back and survey the totality of your life, there's something else to consider. As you've moved through the stages of your existence, have you left the world any different than how you found it?

It's common to tell young people they will change the world, but how often do we actually believe it is possible for ourselves? A lot of doubt can come from misapprehension about what "changing the world" really means. It's true, we can't all go down in history as a famous musician who leaves behind a legacy of breathtaking symphonies. We can't all invent the next lightbulb or electricity or smartphone. While these things have certainly changed the way we live, it's not the only thing that qualifies as world-changing.

When someone comes up to me and tells me I have been a plus in their life, I know I have changed the world. Simply because I have made someone's life better, I have created a better world for myself, my loved ones, and all those who will walk the earth in the future. Creating a positive influence on other people is the most fundamental way to start building your greater impact on the world.

If I had to define impact, I would always start with this idea of positive influence. Has something or someone been transformed by your time, talent, and treasure? Have you invested your resources forward so that people will benefit from them long after your time on earth is over?

On the personal level, impact can consist of adding value to another's life. On a professional level, maybe your leadership has created a program, institution, or organization that reaches many people. Perhaps your impact is environmental, and your work helps to protect and preserve natural resources for future generations. These are all examples of impact you are capable of. So what borders are holding you back?

Circles of Influence

The first border you might be struggling with is a lack of reach. Do you feel that you have lofty goals but no means to attain them? Or even if you have the appropriate resources, perhaps you don't have the platform to find the people who most need help. Regardless of how you feel your reach is limited, there is a solution.

My life purpose is to impact more than one million people in my lifetime. If I achieve that, I will know without a doubt I have had a life well-lived. But you are probably wondering how I could possibly reach so many people. I have a simple strategy to keep my impact ever-expanding and borderless. I view my reach in terms of my circles of influence.

The first circle always starts with self. So often, we view our impact in external terms only. While external impact is the majority of what we pursue, we cannot be kind and influential in others' lives unless we treat ourselves with the same mentality.

This is why impact is the last of the Four Wheels of Life. To live borderless, we first have to make sure we are taking care of our health, relationships, and career, and then we can move towards impacting others positively. So I always start with myself.

Then the next circle of impact would include family and loved ones. Am I positively affecting them every day? Does pursuing my goals make life better for them? Do they have circles of influence that I am not directly a part of? If so, then every time you make the lives of your family members better, you are also benefiting their circles of influence, and your reach grows.

Next, you start at work. If you positively influence your coworkers and do your job well, the company grows. As the company prospers, it impacts people you might have no personal connection to, but as you create a difference in the areas you can reach, it ripples out to affect those you never dreamed you could.

If your goal for influence is more modest than mine, you might be content for your influence to end here. But if we are truly pursuing a Borderless Life, why stop here?

I started to seek more ways to extend my circles of influence. I decided I would write one book per year and take my reach to the next level. Now, whenever someone reads my books, my hope is that they take some idea or inspiration from them that makes a difference in their life. This way, my ability to positively impact others increases exponentially.

Next, in order to reach my goal of one million people, I have to have some way to track my influence. When you start integrating your impact into your life's work, there will always be ways to quantify your reach. I use the number of book sales, the downloads of podcasts I've been on, or even the number of employees I have.

There is no guarantee that every number equals a positive difference made, but it gives me a starting place to know how far I have come and what my next pursuit needs to be in order to reach more people.

When I created IT By Design (ITBD), I wanted to ensure everyone who worked there became better because of their association with the company. When we survey our employees, we are mainly looking for whether they felt it was a good decision to attach themselves to ITBD. Did they align strongly with our values? Has the company influenced their bigger future?

Maybe 80 percent of our current 800 employees answered these questions positively. Now I can count them as people I have impacted, but I can also strive to reach the other 20 percent.

I have also founded a non-profit mentor-mentee program to help others create impacts of their own. We have seven chapters: five in the U.S. and two in India. Fundamentally, it connects entrepreneurs with each other.

Whether people are just beginning their start-ups or have become very successful, they are free to join our community and give back. Those in need can find angel investors or mentors, and those who have something to give find no lack of people to invest in. We go to different temples to find people in need, and we host job fairs where people can find internships.

This is an example of how founding an institution can expand your circles of influence and, more importantly, can continue to positively influence people for generations to come.

Seeing the Need

If you are struggling to find the area of impact you most want to invest in, try observing your community for a while, gathering as much information as you can, and locating where the greatest needs lie. Be curious; it costs nothing.

Even if you are not in a position to fill the whole need all at once, you can still start within your circles of influence and work outward until you have made a community-wide difference.

For example, there was a need in my Sikh community in New Jersey for a bank. The group had never had a financial institution in the country, so I became part of an initiative to establish the first Sikh bank in New Jersey, which will benefit the whole community and set a precedent for what's possible when you see a need and seek to supply the resources for those who need them.

We also have a "Go-Givers" program at ITBD inspired by the book Bob Burg and John David Mann wrote in 2007.[3] We provide opportunities for our employees to take an active role in giving back to the community. First, participants in the program add money to a fund, which the company matches dollar for dollar. We then use that to take meals to homeless shelters in the tri-state area, or in India and the Philippines, we visit orphanages and bring books, stationery, and other goods. Through the program, our employees can build relationships with and become mentors for those we help.

This is another internal company example of seeing a need around you and taking steps to fill it. But here's the key: when you live in such a way to extend your impact, your example can inspire others to create their own impact. For instance, as I have raised my children, I hope to have always set a good example by prioritizing giving back to the community.

My oldest son, Sahib, started volunteering at the Verna Fire Station as a firefighter when he was a freshman at Cornell. He continued his service there for years as a volunteer and eventually became a fire captain.

My middle son, Rohan, started serving as a firefighter as well when he started college in 2024.

My youngest son, Shaan, decided to start a non-profit of his own called A Thread of Hope as a freshman in high school. He recruited his classmates, and they collect unused clothes from different families and other donors to distribute to homeless shelters. He could have let his youth be a border to his impact, but he hasn't. He overcame those doubts and is already building a borderless impact when most have not even considered the importance of doing so.

I have nothing directly to do with the impact my sons have on their community, but because I have pursued impact myself, my passion has compounded through the inspiration I have given my family.

Doing good has a multiplier effect. I always teach that one plus one is not two. It's eleven! Even when you are only able to increase your impact in very small ways, remember that your impact might be growing exponentially without you even noticing, simply because you have inspired others to do the same.

Finally, if you feel that time is the limiting resource holding you back from creating a bigger impact, then you might be in the wrong stage of life at the moment. Be patient.

Remember the Four Wheels. You have 168 PSI to spend on all four, but you do not have to evenly distribute this amount between them. Being in harmony means that you allot a proper amount to each wheel for the period of life you are currently in.

Often, you won't have a lot of time to give to your impact when you are younger. But as long as you are giving some thought to it, you can wait until later in life to hone in on building your impact.

Borderless Lessons from Everest #20

If it feels steep, you're on the right route.

Finding a way to build your impact can be challenging, especially if you are not used to thinking in terms of how you affect the world. Take courage in this: you might not know if you're doing it right, but as long as the way feels steep, you're doing it right. Creating a powerful impact is a journey as difficult as climbing Everest, but if you persist, you will see results.

Best Practices for Borderless Impact

- **Always be curious.** Find out what your community needs, and then determine how you can help. It doesn't cost anything to ask questions and build connections, and you don't know how you might start influencing people without ever knowing it.

- **Start small.** Build up to a larger impact by starting with yourself, moving to your family and friends, your place of work, and then other circles of influence. Take advantage of the ripple effect by beginning programs that others can carry forward.

- **Build evergreen institutions.** When you create an institution, you create a legacy to continue for generations to come.

PART 3

Your Borderless Life

8

The Borderless Vision Starts Now

Living Life By Design

N ow that we have all the necessary tools for each Wheel of Life, we have to take a look at the bigger picture. Remember: To live a Borderless Life, you must live a Life by Design. This means having clarity about your life vision, a plan for exceeding your goals, and a strategy for sticking to it. I call this a Twenty-Year Transformation Plan.

Think of your life like a book. When you're on your last page, whatever age that may be, will you smile reading it? Will you say, "I lived fully. I lived on my terms. I'm proud of this story." That's the real test of a Borderless Life.

Most people never write the story they want. They follow someone else's script, whether it's from their parents, society, or the expectations of others, and then they wonder why they feel unfulfilled.

My Transformation Plan includes living for 125 years. I know I'm not guaranteed that time, but that number challenges me. It stretches how I think about health, purpose, and legacy.

Now it's your turn. What's the number that scares you just enough? If it's 80, what happens if you plan for 100? If it's 90, why not think in terms of 110? Add 20 years to your current horizon, and watch how your decisions change.

That's what it means to live borderless. That's what it means to build a vision worth chasing. Your vision must come before your goals. It is the North Star for your life. Without it, you'll drift as you chase what others want for you instead of what you truly desire.

This is the most important chapter in the book. If you're serious about building a Borderless Life - one that expands your health, relationships, career, and impact beyond limits - you must start with clarity. And clarity starts with vision.

To live a Borderless Life is to live a Life by Design. The framework I'm about to share with you will help you start thinking in terms of design. Allow it to connect your inner world of vision, values, and mindsets with your outer world of goals, systems, and relationships.

It's not enough to set goals. You need to become the person who can live out those goals. This is how we do it.

Step 1: Life Vision Clarity

Create a vivid, emotional, detailed vision of your future self twenty years from now.

Forget "realistic." Dream borderlessly. What does a perfect day look like in twenty years? Where do you wake up? Who are you with? What does your health, work, and impact look like? Picture it all in high definition, or write down a description of this future. This is your North Star.

Now, anchor it by writing a letter from your future self to your current self. This begins to rewire your identity.

After you have established your vision, you must clarify your purpose. Before you set any goals or even identify your values, you must know *why* any of it matters. As Simon Sinek teaches in his classic framework, *Start With Why,* people don't buy *what* you do; they buy *why* you do it.[4] The same is true for your own goals. Purpose gives your vision emotional weight. It becomes your inner engine during hard seasons and your compass when priorities compete.

I've already shared that my purpose is to be a plus—a positive impact—in over one million lives. That includes my family, friends, team members, clients, strategic partners, podcast listeners, social followers, book readers, and those impacted by my non-profit. Every decision I make must move that number forward. That's the kind of purpose that pulls you out of bed and through adversity.

Your purpose doesn't have to be perfect. But it has to be yours. Ask yourself these questions to start to define your purpose:

- What mission would still matter to me if no one applauded it?

- Who do I feel called to serve or elevate?

- What pain have I experienced that I want to turn into purpose?

Next, write down one sentence that starts with "My purpose is to. . . ." Reread that sentence every week. Let it be your lighthouse through fog and fatigue.

Reflection Questions:

- If I stayed on my current path, where would I end up in twenty years?

- What would I regret if I didn't change anything now?

- Who must I become to live that future vision?

Step 2: Core Values Clarity

Your core values are the compass for your decisions. You don't just live your values when life is easy. You live them when things get hard. That's why you must choose five personal values that matter most and define what they look like in action.

Mine are Humility, Accountability, Positivity, Passion, and Your Community. Together, they form my H.A.P.P.Y. code. Your own values don't need to form a catchy acronym, but they do need to be important enough to show up in your daily life, especially under stress.

Reflection Questions:

- What do I want to be known for—by those who matter most?

- When have I felt most "in alignment" with my values?

- What behavior shows that I am living this value?

Step 3: Core Mindsets Inventory

Mindsets are the operating system of your future self. I have intentionally cultivated these mindsets to live borderlessly:

Health, Gratitude, Positive Focus, Grit, Resilience, Courage, Commitment, Growth, Curiosity, Lifelong Learning, Go-Giver, Abundance, Borderless Thinking, and Relationship-First.

For your own mindsets, what matters most is to pick the top three that will shape your next chapter. Go deep, not wide.

Reflection Questions:

- Which mindsets have powered my biggest wins in life?

- Which ones do I admire in others but haven't fully developed yet?

- What mindset would change everything for me right now?

Step 4: Guiding Principles for Way of Life

Your guiding principles are about your how: How you speak, how you listen, how you resolve tension, how you love.

Your way of life principles guide your behavior across all relationships. Here are some of mine:

- **Active Listening:** Seek to understand before being understood.

- **Appreciating Others:** Celebrate wins, efforts, and presence.

- **Sharing and Caring:** Be generous with time, wisdom, and empathy.

These principles build trust, emotional safety, and collaboration—in family, teams, and communities.

Reflection Questions:

- What do I want people to experience when they interact with me?

- How do I respond when I'm triggered or challenged?

- What principles do I want to model for my kids, team, or spouse?

Step 5: Your Twenty-Year Transformation Plan

Now that you have the internal compass, it's time to chart the external path. With this final step, you can design a timeline to guide the rest of your life. This will include:

- **20-Year Vision**: Your Borderless Life Future

- **10-Year Milestone**: Halfway markers of identity and success

- **5-Year Leap**: New foundation for health, wealth, and relationships

- **3-Year Build**: Real traction and visibility

- **1-Year Action**: SMART goals aligned to your vision

- **90-Day Sprint**: Where focus meets execution

We'll start with the big picture: twenty years. Creating this timeline begins with a candid assessment of where you are right now.

- What is the status of your health? How is your mind, body, and soul? Are things as you want them to be, or are there pain points?

- How healthy are your relationships? Are you consistently growing closer to those around you, or does the influence of others limit you?

- Are you growing at your job? Is your financial picture stagnant? Are you learning new skills and information?

- What is your current impact? How many circles of influence can you currently reach? Are there any institutions or programs that will continue beyond your own lifespan?

At first, all you need to do is answer these questions as honestly as you can. Do not make judgments about whether the answers are good or bad; simply capture a full picture of your life and how much time you are investing in each Wheel.

Next, look twenty years into the future. If your life is continuously expanding, uninhibited by any borders or self-limiting beliefs, what will your life look like then? Take each of the Four Wheels, one at a time, and create a new picture of your life and activities. What is the best future you can imagine?

Now it's time to assess the difference between your current existence and your twenty-year vision. What needs to change within five years in each area of life in order to reach the twenty-year goal? What needs to be true in ten years? Fifteen? Take time to dive into the details. How old will you be in ten or fifteen years? What will that mean for your career or relationships? How will it affect your health or impact?

I've included a sample of the worksheet I use myself and with my own employees. This is a big picture worksheet, but it is so important to use as a reference and reminder that you have designed your future. When you're tempted to give in to a border or allow self-doubt to limit you, remember that borders are default. Breaking borders is design.

IT BY DESIGN

LIFE BY DESIGN PLAN

Wheels of Life	1 Year	5 Years	10 Years	15 Years	20 Years
#HealthByDesign					
Physical Life					
Mental Life					
Spiritual Life					
#RelationshipsByDesign					
Family Life					
Friends Life					
Social Life					
#CareerByDesign					
Work Life					
Financial Life					
Intellectual Life					
#ImpactByDesign					
Service Life					
Impact Life					
Succession Life					

After you have completed a twenty-year plan, it's time to get specific. I have created worksheets and goal trackers to help you with quarterly and yearly goals in each Wheel of Life. For example, I will walk you through the health goal trackers I use.

As you create an annual plan for your health goals, use your twenty-year plan to set up achievable goals for the end of the year. These should work toward your larger goals in measurable ways.

For example, if you want to be able to run a marathon, perhaps you want to train for a half-marathon by the end of the year. If you want to cut sugar out of your diet, start by limiting your sugar consumption to only the weekends or every other day. Be consistent with the small goals, and you will see marked differences as you strive toward bigger goals.

The next step is to make sure you know why these goals are important to you. If you don't have a good reason, it is that much harder to stay motivated. Again, you also need to acknowledge the current reality of your situation so you can track your progress with clarity.

Finally, take a look around. What resources do you have access to that will help you achieve your goal? In terms of health, this might consist of fitness classes, a gym membership, a counselor, or accountability friends who have similar goals. You do not live in a vacuum, and your efforts don't have to be unsupported either.

IT
DESIGN

HEALTH BY DESIGN – GOAL TRACKER

Annual Plan

1-Year Goal	IMPORTANCE: What makes this goal so significant to you?	What's the reality of your current situation?	What resources and people are available to support you?
1.			
2.			
3.			
4.			
5.			

Finally, we break the goals down even further into a tracker for the next quarter. This is where your Life by Design can get practical. What are you doing on a daily basis to achieve your goals? Make sure your goal is SMART: specific, measurable, achievable, relevant, and time-based. This will ensure that you make real progress.

If your goal is not specific enough, you will not be able to take direct action to achieve it. If it is not measurable, you won't know if you have made progress, and you will get discouraged more quickly. If it is not achievable, the goal becomes a border rather than a means to break borders, and you are setting yourself up to fail. If it is not relevant to your twenty-year plan, then you might be driving your Car of Needs in some direction, but it might not be the direction you want to go. Finally, if your goal is not time-based, you will have trouble sticking to your plan in the long run.

Identifying obstacles to your goal and strategies to overcome those obstacles will also help you make progress. I've provided some strategies already that you might want to try if you come across a particularly difficult blockage in your path.

Lastly, when it comes to your quarterly assessment, write down milestones or specific achievements you have accomplished or will accomplish in the next quarter. They don't need to be major, but simply acknowledging your victories boosts your confidence and breaks the borders of self-doubt that hold you back.

IT BY
DESIGN

HEALTH BY DESIGN – GOAL TRACKER
Next Quarter

S.M.A.R.T. Goals	Obstacles	Strategies	Specific milestone/action
1.			
2.			
3.			
4.			
5.			

If you want to use the goal trackers I have created, go to https://sunnyspeaks.net. There are trackers and goal worksheets for every Wheel of Life. You can also use the questions I have written in this book to direct your own life assessments. Either way, be deliberate about creating your goals and moving steadily toward them, and you will be well on your way to a Borderless Life.

As you start to implement your Twenty-Year Transformation Plan, remember to review every ninety days, celebrate wins, learn from losses, adjust where necessary, and stay focused. Above all else, remember to live by design, not default.

Reflection Questions:

- If I fully owned my power, what would I achieve in twenty years?

- What one goal this quarter would move the needle most?

- Where am I over-complicating things? What can I simplify?

You now have the tools to build your Borderless Life Vision. But this chapter only works if you work it. Don't let it be the chapter you read and forget. Let it be the one you return to, live by, and expand through.

Your future self is waiting.

Let's go build the vision.

50 Borderless Lessons from Everest

1. Every mountain has ten peaks inside it.

2. You carry capability, not comfort.

3. Comfort is not the goal—clarity is.

4. The climb reveals what comfort conceals.

5. Commitment is day one. Consistency is day one hundred.

6. You train for Everest long before Base Camp.

7. Climbing is a mindset, not a trail.

8. Mind follows altitude. So does emotion.

9. Stillness reveals the next move.

10. You don't conquer Everest. You align with it.

11. Every step either elevates or exhausts.

12. You don't rise alone—teams elevate together.

13. One slow teammate sets the pace.

14. Lifelong Learning makes every step lighter.

15. If you're not elevating, you're not progressing.

16. Slow is smooth. Smooth is fast.

17. Courage starts the climb. Grit finishes it.

18. Walking flat means walking in circles.

19. Your next step must be higher.

20. If it feels steep, you're on the right route.

21. Fear is just future imagined.

22. If you can't see the peak, trust the path.

23. Growth begins where breath gets short.

24. Test altitude before you chase altitude.

25. Nature doesn't care. Climb anyway.

26. Altitude strips ego. Only effort remains.

27. Discipline is louder than motivation.

28. You reach Everest by breaking inner borders.

29. You are what you rehearse.

30. Resilience is built, not born.

31. Mountains don't move, mindsets do.

32. My son walked beside me. My purpose led us.

33. Going up means going through.

34. The summit humbles. The trail shapes.

35. You're strongest at your most uncertain step.

36. Borderless living means fearless committing.

37. The mission chooses who finishes it.

38. Gear helps. Grit wins.

39. Altitude changes oxygen and outlook.

40. Clarity grows in oxygen debt.

41. Progress isn't forward. It's upward.

42. Anxiety = elevation + imagination.

43. Your elevation is in your effort.

44. Preparation is humility in action.

45. Pain is the price of perspective.

46. Breath is wisdom. Listen to it.

47. A flat path builds nothing.

48. One step. One breath. One border broken.

49. Mountains test belief, not just legs.

50. Borderless life begins where the air gets thin.

Endnotes

1   To learn more about outsourcing and offshore success, check out my book *The Secret to Building Winning Global Teams: How to Leverage Offshore Talent to Exponentially Increase Profitability and Valuation*

2   Aanstoos, Christopher M. "Maslow's Hierarchy of Needs." *EBSCO*, 2024. https://www.ebsco.com/research-starters/psychology/maslows-hierarchy-needs. Accessed 14 May 2025.

3   Burg, Bob, and John David Mann. "The Go-Giver: A Little Story About A Powerful Business Idea." Portfolio, 2007.

4   Sinek, Simon. *Start with Why: How Great Leaders Inspire Everyone to Take Action*. Portfolio, 2011.

About the Author

Sunny Kaila is the embodiment of the American Dream. He is a TEDx speaker, entrepreneur, and bestselling author. As the Founder and CEO of IT By Design, he has built a leading global talent solutions provider for managed service providers (MSPs). With an unwavering entrepreneurial spirit, Sunny possesses a unique ability to identify opportunities amidst challenges and embrace calculated risks when the time calls for a leap of faith. His remarkable journey from an immigrant to a successful tech industry leader is a testament to his determination and vision.

Connect with Sunny at SunnySpeaks.net

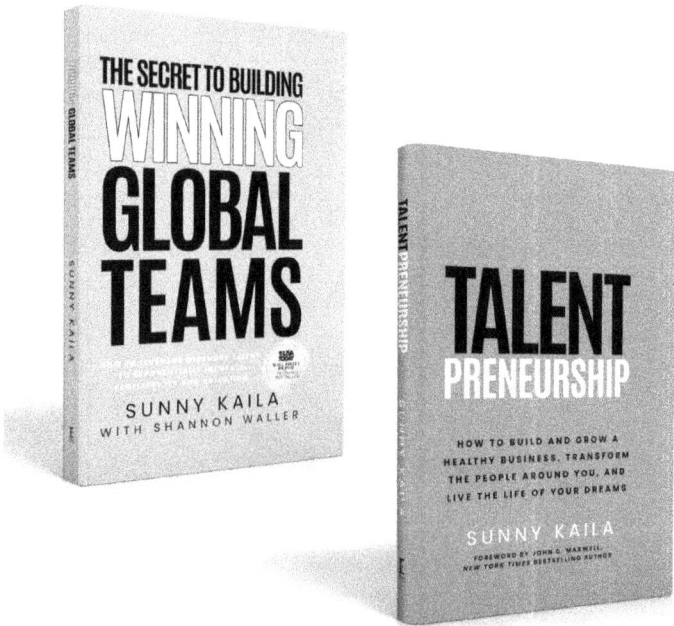

CONNECT WITH SUNNY

Follow him on your favorite social media platforms today.

@SunnyKaila

@ItByDesign

@IT_BY_DESIGN

@it.by.design

@ItByDesign

ITBD.NET

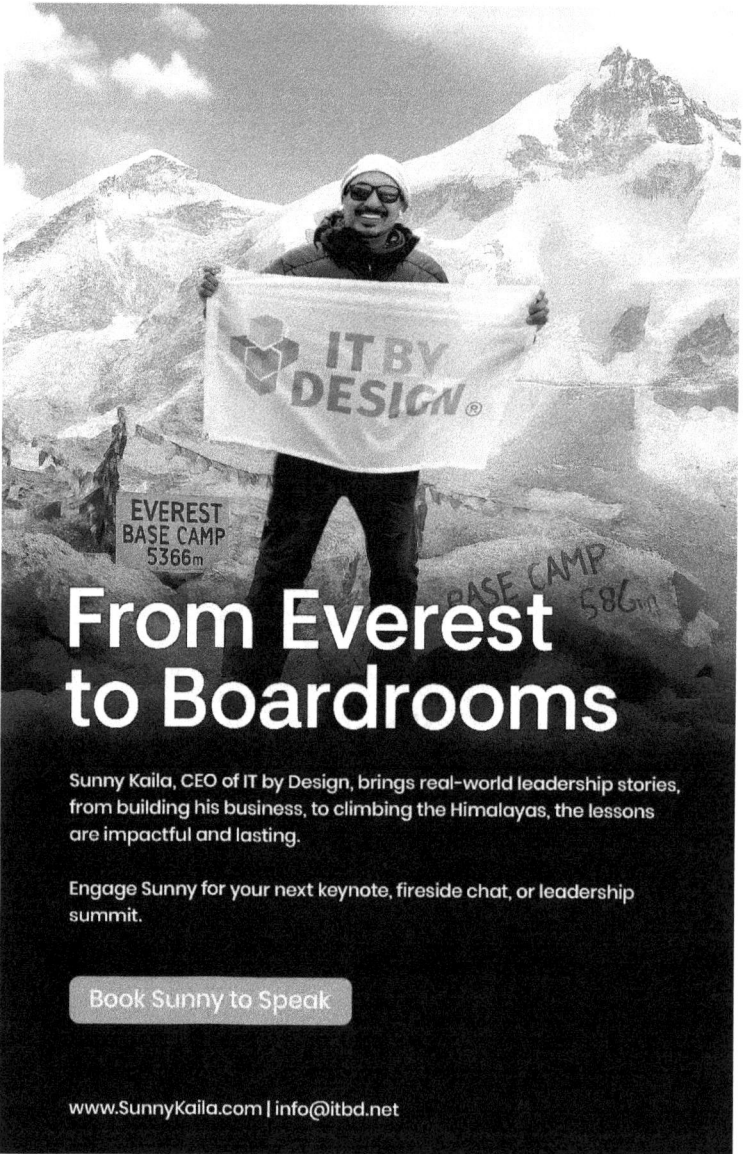

From Everest to Boardrooms

Sunny Kaila, CEO of IT by Design, brings real-world leadership stories, from building his business, to climbing the Himalayas, the lessons are impactful and lasting.

Engage Sunny for your next keynote, fireside chat, or leadership summit.

Book Sunny to Speak

www.SunnyKaila.com | info@itbd.net